Vintage Christmas Greetings

COLORING BOOK

Marty Noble

Dover Publications, Inc.
Mineola, New York

Rare, early twentieth century greeting cards are the inspiration for these wonderful scenes celebrating Christmas. Thirty one different illustrations are ready for you to color including old-fashioned, chubby-cheeked Santas delivering toys, horse-drawn sleigh rides, children decorating the tree, and many other seasonal images. Use colored pencils, crayons, or markers to color the pages. Color them any way you like and give them to friends and family to spread a little Christmas cheer.

Copyright

Copyright © 2014 by Dover Publications, Inc.
All rights reserved.

Bibliographical Note

Creative Haven Vintage Christmas Greetings Coloring Book, first published by Dover Publications, Inc., in 2014, contains all of the artwork from *Vintage Christmas Greetings Coloring Book* (2011) and one additional plate, all by artist Marty Noble.

International Standard Book Number

ISBN-13: 978-0-486-79189-0
ISBN-10: 0-486-79189-0

Manufactured in the United States by RR Donnelley
79189009   2015
www.doverpublications.com

Sing a song of Christmas,
    A bag of Christmas toys-
Santa Claus is bringing them
    To little girls and boys,
When the bag is opened
    Won't the kiddies shout,
And then they play all
    Christmas day
And scatter things about.

Merry Christmas

May all thy hours
be winged with joy

May Christmas bring
you loads of joy

A MERRY CHRISTMAS TO YOU

Christmas Greetings